Dieses Heft enthält 25 Kopiervorlagen:

- **10 Vocabulary Action Sheets (+ Lösungen)**
- **15 Language Action Sheets (+ Lösungen)**

Vocabulary Action Sheets (VAS):

Sichere Wortschatzkenntnisse sind nur zu erreichen, wenn die eingeführten und „gelernten" Wörter und Wendungen regelmäßig wiederholt, geübt und kontrolliert werden. Die VAS ermöglichen – unitweise – eine motivierende Beschäftigung mit dem erlernten Wortschatz: Die Schülerinnen und Schüler (S) entschlüsseln die einzusetzenden Vokabeln mithilfe von Kurzdefinitionen, vervollständigen kurze Beispielsätze, üben Wortschatz nach Wortfeldern, suchen Gegensatzpaare, versprachlichen Bilder. Auf diese Weise wird der zu beherrschende Wortschatz besser vernetzt und gespeichert, als es durch die alleinige Beschäftigung mit den Vokabellisten des Schülerbuches geschehen kann.

Zu jeder Unit des Schülerbuches **English G • Access 4** stehen jeweils zwei VAS mit dem größten Teil des produktiv zu beherrschenden Wortschatzes zur Verfügung.

Language Action Sheets (LAS):

Zu jeder Unit des Schülerbuches **English G • Access 4** werden zwei bis vier LAS angeboten, mit denen die S die zentralen grammatischen Strukturen erarbeiten und/oder festigen können.

Die LAS beginnen in der Regel mit einem Abschnitt, der die S auf eine oder mehrere Seiten im Schülerbuch **English G • Access 4** verweist. Mithilfe der genannten Stellen im Schülerbuch vervollständigen die S zunächst Sätze oder kurze Dialoge, die die zu erarbeitende grammatische Struktur enthalten.

Je nach grammatischem Phänomen komplettieren die S anschließend Paradigmen, machen sich grammatische Bildungs- und Funktions-Regularitäten bewusst und vergleichen ggf. mit verwandten grammatischen Phänomenen. Dabei werden sie kleinschrittig angeleitet durch zweisprachige Arbeitsanweisungen zu den einzelnen LAS-Abschnitten.

Jedes LAS endet mit einem Verweis auf den zugehörigen *Grammar File*-Abschnitt des Schülerbuches.

Die LAS können im Rahmen des flexiblen Grammatikkonzepts von **English G • Access** anstelle der *Looking at language*-Abschnitte des Schülerbuches zum Einsatz kommen (zu den Einsatzorten der LAS siehe die Inhaltsübersicht auf der nächsten Seite). Am Ende des Schuljahres halten die S eine selbst erstellte Elementargrammatik in Händen, die sie auch dann noch zum Nachschlagen und Wiederholen nutzen können, wenn sie ihre ausgeliehenen Schülerbücher zurückgegeben haben.

Vocabulary Action Sheets:

VAS	Einsatzort	VAS	Einsatzort
1.1	nach Unit 1	4.1	nach Unit 4
1.2	nach Unit 1	4.2	nach Unit 4
2.1	nach Unit 2	5.1	nach Unit 5
2.2	nach Unit 2	5.2	nach Unit 5
3.1	nach Unit 3		
3.2	nach Unit 3		

Language Action Sheets:

LAS	Thema	Einsatzort
1.1	The gerund as subject and object	Unit 1, S. 20
1.2	The gerund after prepositions	Unit 1, S. 20
2.1	REVISION Conditional sentences (types 1 and 2)	Unit 2, S. 37
2.2	Conditional sentences (type 3)	Unit 2, S. 42
2.3	Countable and uncountable nouns	Unit 2, S. 47
3.1	The passive: different tenses	Unit 3, S. 58
3.2	The passive of verbs with two objects	Unit 3, S. 62
3.3	The *to*-infinitive	Unit 3, S. 58
4.1	REVISION Indirect speech: statements	Unit 4, S. 76
4.2	Indirect speech: questions	Unit 4, S. 84
4.3	Indirect speech: commands, requests, advice, suggestions	Unit 4, S. 90
4.4	The definite article	Unit 4, S. 86
5.1	REVISION Relative clauses	Unit 5, S. 97/110
5.2	The present participle (I)	Unit 5, S. 97
5.3	The present participle (II)	Unit 5, S. 104

Lösungen VAS

Lösungen LAS

	Big cities	Verbs	Pictures	German/ English	American English words	Context
1	Big cities, like NYC or London, are divided into b_____ s_____.	From our campsite, we were able to hear the waterfall r_____.		Aufnahme, Foto; Einstellung, Szene s_____	BE: flat AE: a_____	His flat is quite c_____ l_____, near the main station.
2	The fastest way to go around is by s_____. (BE: underground).	Did the police a_____ the thief?		künstlich, Kunst- m_____-	BE: biscuit AE: c_____	The Statue of L_____ is near Manhattan.
3	Usually, there is a central s_____ where people meet.	If you l_____ too far out of the window, you might fall!		klasse, großartig a_____	BE: rubbish AE: g_____	A spoon is usually made of m_____ or plastic.
4	People live in tall apartment b_____ s_____.	Oh no! Why does this program always c_____?		Zoll (2,54 cm) i_____	BE: queue AE: l_____	When I travel, I have all my things in my b_____.
5	Some of the buildings have twenty or more s_____ s_____.	This roof might c_____ if there is too much snow on it.		Ich sollte lieber ... I'_____ ...	BE: trousers AE: p_____	Life u_____ be harder two hundred years ago.
6	That's why they all have e_____ s_____ (BE: lifts).	Do you m_____ if John smokes?		Ich denke ... / Ich nehme an ... I g_____ ...	BE: pavement AE: s_____	That basketball player is almost seven f_____ tall!
7	Some streets are big a_____ s_____ with shops and trees.	Use your mouse to c_____ on the link.		Spinner/in w_____	BE: shop AE: s_____	In winter we go to the i_____ swimming pool.
8	Do you live in the centre or in a s_____ of a big city?	She is going to b_____ a cake for his birthday.		Vorschlag s_____	BE: holiday AE: v_____	What is the d_____ between an adverb and an adjective?

	American spelling	Verbs	Pictures	German/ English	Small words	Context
1	BE: centre AE: ____	I can't p____ computers – I only use them.	(illustration) s____	Typ, Kerl g____	At the weekend she often hangs ____ with her friends.	I felt quite i____ when he said I was stupid.
2	BE: colour AE: ____	What a nice day. Let's t____ a walk!	(illustration)	legendär, berühmt l____	Are you afraid ____ sharks?	Her mum puts a lot of p____ on her to do better at school.
3	BE: travelled AE: ____	It looks nice when all the flowers b____ in spring.	(illustration)	Meine / Sehr geehrte Damen und Herren L____	Well, I wouldn't like to get too close ____ a shark!	That was a clever m____ – now you've won the game!
4	BE: metre AE: ____	How would you a____ his presentation? – I think it was good!	(illustration)	Zeitmesser t____	Let's go! I'm not very keen ____ watching this show.	Spain is nice, but I can't s____ the hot temperatures in summer.
5	BE: favourite AE: ____	Now let's d____ the class into four groups.	(illustration)	dessen, deren w____	The building was so old that they decided to tear it ____.	Don't try to cross the r____ tracks here – it's really dangerous!
6	BE: travelling AE: ____	Which part of the text does your question r____ to?	(illustration)	Samen s____	That museum has lots of interesting works ____ art.	We could eat at my place – I still have some f____ pizza.
7	BE: theatre AE: ____	She liked that boy, so she tried to m____ eye contact.	(illustration)	Ausschuss, Rat c____	After the discussion we moved ____ to the next point on the list.	Did you see their concert on TV? It was a great p____.
8	BE: neighbour AE: ____	If things go wrong, you shouldn't try to k____ to the plan.	(illustration)	Vortragsweise d____	Can you sum ____ the main points of the discussion?	On some German roads there is no speed l____.

	Adjectives	Cooking	Context	Definitions	Verbs	Pictures	American English	German/ English
1	You want to swim from Britain to France? You must be c___ !	What's you favourite d___ ? – Fish and chips.	This isn't just a storm – it's a h___ !	very wet ground, sometimes with water and plants: s___	When you f___ water, it turns to ice.		BE: cinema AE: m___ t	Karnevalsfeiern in New Orleans M___ G___
2	This toilet is so dirty – it's d___ !	I'd love to make a cake, but I don't have all the i___ s.	More than 200 years ago, America was a British c___ .	informal English for 'kind of': k___	It's difficult to c___ a job and a family.		BE: wardrobe AE: c___	sowohl … als auch … b___ … …?
3	I know. This is what most p___ toilets are like.	Water b___ s at 100 degrees Celsius.	The temperature is forty d___ s.	the first people in America: N___ A___ s	The best way to cook this fish is to f___ it in hot oil.		BE: jewellery AE: j___	Warum probierst du nicht …? W___ n___ t___ …?
4	No cream for me, please. I'm a___ to dairy products.	Use a normal s___ to boil the potatoes first.	40°? Do you mean C___ or Fahrenheit?	meat that comes from a cow: b___	Why don't you r___ the chicken in the oven?		BE: in the centre of NYC AE: in d___ NYC	Ich hätte auch geschrien. I w___ s___ h___ too.
5	Be careful. That knife is very s___ .	Then fry the potatoes in a good f___ p___ .	She was so tired she went s___ to bed.	my grandfather's father is my: g___ - g___	I'm hungry. Can you r___ a good restaurant?		BE: (public) toilet AE: r___	Honig / Schätzchen h___
6	Now, wait a minute! Don't be so i___ .	You need an o___ to bake the cake.	Most of the s___ s in America came from Europe.	sb. who speaks a language as their first language: n___ s___	Do you f___ coming to the cinema with us?		BE: (small, cheap) restaurant AE: d___	Er hatte es selbst getötet. He had killed it h___
7	Our teacher is very s___ . We're not allowed to talk in class.	Her meals always taste great. She's a very good c___ .	I wear my best suit only on special o___ s.	material from a plant that is used to make clothes: c___	Your guitar sounds terrible. You should t___ it first.		BE: tram AE: s___	in der ganzen Stadt a___ o___ c___
8	The letters were so t___ that she couldn't read them.	Most children love spaghetti with tomato s___ .	It's better to use t___ tomatoes for the soup.	There are 100 c___ s in a metre.	Oh yes, I forgot to t___ the strings!		BE: lift AE: e___	Muster p___

#	The fourth word	Food	Context	Blacks in America	Verbs	Pictures	Writing a text	German/English
1	formal – dollar / informal – / b____	You put all the ingredients in one big pot to make a / s____.	Don't use too much curry / p____. It's too hot!	____ 1960s, blacks didn't have the same rights as whites.	Does this dog / b____ you? Dogs are not allowed in here.		I like that author's / s____. His stories are always funny.	Preiselbeere / c____
2	new – fashion / old – / t____	I love parsley. It's my favourite / h____.	Is rainy weather / t____ of Wales?	Blacks couldn't go to some public places: there was / s____.	Bullies sometimes / b____ u____ other students.	a ____ of books	Don't repeat the same word too often. Use a / s____.	Verstand, Sinn, Geist / m____
3	cow – beef / pig – / p____	Pepper is a very well-known / s____.	Today is Jill's / w____ day. She's marrying Tom.	Whites often had / p____ s____ against blacks.	He tried to / m____ his wife, but she survived.		Only write down information that is / r____ to the topic.	ein bisschen, etwas / a l____
4	beef/pork – meat / milk/butter – / d____ / p____	If you don't keep fresh milk cool, it turns / s____.	Don't say / r____ fast. It's more correct to say *really* fast.	Restaurants and cinemas practiced / d____ against blacks.	Do you always / s____ o____ if you don't agree with someone?		This sentence is too difficult. I would / p____ it.	beschränkt, begrenzt / l____
5	cinema – programme / restaurant – / m____	Dark chocolate does not really taste sweet but / b____.	A lot of ships have small, / r____ windows.	Sometimes blacks were c____ ed n____ in the street.	Some people still / h____ animals to eat them.		People should get your main points even if they just / s____ your text.	Leder / l____
6	night – day / dark blue – / l____ blue	Indian food is often too / h____ for Europeans.	I don't know what to do. Can you give me some / a____?	But more and more people had the c____ to speak out.	Suddenly an idea / f____ ed through my mind.		The h____ often tells you what a text is about.	mittelgroß; mittel- / m____
7	ball – round / egg – o____	This soup isn't very / s____. It tastes like water.	You need official / p____ to hunt alligators.	Many students joined the c____ r____ protests.	The police decided to s____ the dog because it had bitten people.		And the s____ – s____ give you more details.	Tierwelt, frei lebende Tiere / w____
8	freeze at 0° – Celsius / freeze at 32° – / F____	How about some apple p____ for dessert?	We live in a small flat. It's only about fifty s____ metres.	Even for today's g____ there are still some problems.	The bridge was destroyed in the war, so they had to r____ it.	a t____ r____ clock	Use photos or g____ if sth. is difficult to describe.	Dokumentarfilm / d____

	A wildfire	Pictures	Context	Opposites	Definitions	Verbs	German/English
1	Last week, a fire started in a nature r_____ in California.	d_____	They had nothing in common – they were c_____ different.	comfortable – u_____	a picture you have in your head: i_____	If your back hurts, lie down and s_____ .	die Woche zuvor the w_____ b_____
2	It soon became an e_____ s for people in the area.		There's always a big c_____ between rich and poor people.	(to) ask for directions – (to) g_____ directions	if sth. is not from your country, it's: f_____	She was at the party too, but he didn't s_____ t_____ her.	Wie bitte? s_____ ?
3	Some r_____ s had to be evacuated.	P _____ (AE)/ _____ (BE)	I love the sea. I want to become a m_____ scientist.	(to) interview people together – (to) interview people s_____	a person you don't know: s_____	We tried to l_____ o_____ for you in the crowd, but we couldn't see you.	Ich möchte, dass du mir hilfst. I'd l_____ y_____ help me.
4	At first, the fire seemed u_____ .		A lot of young people use s_____ media to stay in contact.	legal – i_____	a woman who invites guests: h_____	Does that charity s_____ poor people?	Sprichwort, Redensart s_____
5	So the local f_____ d had to call for help.		It was so dark you couldn't see anything a_____ .	(to) let sth. happen – (to) p_____ sth.	12 o'clock in the middle of the day: n_____	The man who helped them didn't want to r_____ his name.	Ökologie e_____
6	But the fire is out now, leaving huge b_____ areas.	_____ (AE)/ _____ (BE)	Michael is a c_____ name both in Britain and Germany.	cause – e_____	the natural world in which everything lives: e_____	She's really good at maths, so she t_____ s other students.	Mir ist schwindelig. I'm f_____ f_____ .
7	The c_____ of the fire is not yet known.		What was her r_____ to the news? – Well, she was shocked.	dangerous – s_____	a person who knows a lot about a special topic: e_____	Can you help me to s_____ u_____ my new TV?	obwohl a_____
8	In California, there are often wildfires because of d_____ s.		An audition for a film doesn't go fast. It's actually a long p_____ .	impossible – p_____	an official document that allows you to do sth.: p_____	If you're not happy at work, why don't you s_____ jobs?	Zitat q_____ / q_____

English G Access I 4 Vocabulary & Language Action Sheets   Illustrationen: Roland Beier, Berlin

	Hollywood	Pictures	Context	Adjectives	The fourth word	Verbs	German/English
1	Beverly Hills near Hollywood is the home of many c _____ s.		Everything stays the same in my village. There's just no c _____ !	I love baby seals. They're so c _____ !	BE – queue AE – l _____	Some parents p _____ their children on the head when they're doing well.	Entdeckung d _____
2	You might see a film star near the v _____ lounge of a Hollywood hotel.		So how are you enjoying your s _____ in the US?	He gave a calm and d _____ speech at the funeral.	writing – (to) spell speaking – (to) p _____	Today, with Twitter and the internet, news g _____ v _____ in a few minutes.	das Neueste the l _____
3	But often you can't because there are s _____ guards.		The sun, sea and beach give Ibiza a very relaxed a _____ .	I'm sure we will win tonight. I'm quite o _____ about that.	April – month autumn – s _____	When did Columbus d _____ America? – I think it was in 1492.	Bleib(t) auf dem Laufenden! S _____ p _____ .
4	In Hollywood, the film team set up the next t _____		What shall I say? Is she a Mrs or a M _____ Smith?	He was wearing his best suit and s _____ black shoes.	(to) decide – decision (to) explain – e _____	There was a fire, so they had to e _____ the building	Meilen pro Stunde m _____ p _____ h _____ (m _____)
5	The actor read the s _____ to prepare for the next scene.		Do you have the p _____ to swim more than one kilometre?	The new Rolls-Royce is a really p _____ car.	wind – (to) blow river – (to) f _____	They were brothers, but they didn't h _____ much in common.	Ich fühle mit / Mein Mitgefühl gilt … M _____ h _____ g _____ o _____ to …
6	They were filming the third s _____ of a famous sitcom.		In the rainforest, we were completely c _____ o _____ from the outside world.	His wife often starts crying. She's very e _____ .	BE – year ten AE – t _____ g _____	Did the police i _____ the cause of the fire?	Präfix, Vorsilbe p _____
7	That sitcom is one of many comedy p _____ s on TV.		It is getting warmer because the earth's c _____ is changing.	I'm on nobody's side. I'm n _____ .	city – skyline countryside – l _____	When you c _____ their stories, you will find big differences.	Gliederung o _____
8	It will also be shown in Britain on c _____ 4.		What's the o _____ of good? – Bad.	The song is really c _____ .I just can't get it out of my head!	(to) burn – burnt (to) relax – r _____	When you crossed the border, did you e _____ any problems?	in Kürze / in wenigen Worten b _____

#	Adjectives	South Dakota	Context	Definitions	Verbs	Pictures	American English	German/English
1	Badlands are very dry and d____.	Not many plants grow in the South Dakota B____.	Where are my keys? I must have them s____!	the sound you hear when feet touch the ground: f____	She was angry and s____ her books down on the table.		BE: worktop AE: c____	Kein Wunder. N____ w____.
2	The service is not only good – it's e____!	A large area of South Dakota is just p____.	£10 is just the meal. We'll have to pay e____ for the drinks.	the way you feel in a situation: m____	He was driving very slowly, so the cars behind started to h____.		BE: drinking fountain AE: w____ f____	sprechend t____
3	Don't be so g____. It's not the end of the world!	There are some r____ s____ for Native Americans.	A thief is a person who steals other people's p____.	a way of doing something, using special skills: t____	She t____ed the bag under her arm and left.		BE: lesson AE: p____	es erfordert Übung i____ t____ p____
4	The Black Hills are s____ to the Lakota.	Most of them are from the Lakota t____ s____.	Stealing things is against the l____.	able to speak two languages like a native speaker: b____	Didn't your doctor a____ you to stop smoking?		BE: mark AE: g____	ob w____
5	That was really h____ to leave the baby crying for hours.	C____ with the Lakota started when US settlers moved west.	This is the only thing you can do. You don't have a c____.	the person who brings you a message: m____	Come on, we're late! Can't you s____ a bit?		BE: driving licence AE: d____ l____	in den letzten Jahren in r____ y____
6	The language of this rap song is quite o____.	South Dakota is often sunny with a c____ sky.	That was quite an i____ to her when you said she was too stupid.	to come back or go back: (to) r____	We lost the match, so we didn't q____ for the finals.		BE: head teacher AE: p____	sowieso a____
7	It was great – we had a w____ time.	A popular event with horses is a r____.	The four presidents' g____ faces are on Mount Rushmore.	any day except Saturday and Sunday: w____	Has she gone home? I didn't n____ her leave!		BE: per cent AE: p____	aus diesem Grund f____ t____ r____
8	I wouldn't drink that water. It's f____.	I love watching horses g____.	Most of us think that the t____es we have to pay are too high.	the activity of telling stories: s____	Suddenly she c____ to him and asked him to dance.		BE: (to) give sb. a lift AE: (to) give sb. a r____	auch wenn; obwohl e____ t____

	The fourth word	Mount Rushmore	Context	School in the USA	Verb phrases	Small words	Verbs	German/English
1	noisy – noise / silent – s___	The presidents' heads in the Black Hills are made of g___.	The s___ is really bad. The waiters are so unfriendly!	Reading out all the names from the r___ is called roll-call.	l___ sb. a book / a CD / money	You can do an internet search ___ more information.	Did you p___ the test? – Yes, I got Grade A!	nicht länger; nicht mehr / n___ (...) a___ l___
2	class – teacher / football team – c___	When did they c___ those heads on Mount Rushmore?	I'm so tired I can h___ keep my eyes open.	If you like reading books, a course in l___ is ideal for you.	c___ a king / a queen	It's a small town – you often run ___ people you know.	He tried to stay, but the police f___ed him to leave.	mehr als an jedem anderen Ort / *more t___ a___ other place / in*
3	good – bad / (to) pass – (to) f___	The memorial was paid for with t___ s'___ money.	Which p___ are you playing in our school play?	Learn how people live together in s___ s___.	t___ c___ *of* a child / a sick person / your old grandmother	It's not very easy to hunt ___ horseback.	At first she wanted to go, but then she c___ed her mind.	ziemlich / f___
4	(to) help – help / (to) support – s___	It led to bad r___ with the Lakota.	They have a good r___. They get on quite well.	In the US, students are often given a___ s___.	i___ a new system / a new law / a new program	Do you like the American way ___ life?	It's not allowed to s___ the walls with graffiti.	aber; allerdings; jedoch / h___
5	never – always / at no time – *at a___* t___	Most of them find the memorial e___ offensive.	That car is more powerful. Its e___ is much bigger.	You have to know the rules if you want to *a___* a course.	g___ a country / a tribe / a colony	This song is dedicated ___ my mother.	When she's sad, she g___s out of the window for hours.	Totale, Totalaufnahme / l___ s___
6	France – country / Europe – c___	Some people see it as a monument to American p___.	They're such a bad team – it's not s___ that they lost.	Students who are often late have to attend extra s___ s___.	m___ house / flat	Do all Americans show so much pride ___ their country?	You're doing it really well. Just k___ up the good work!	Halbtotale / m___ s___
7	powerful – power / strong – s___	There's an evening c___ with floodlights.	So the m___ of the story is: always help other people!	You need written permission to leave the school g___.	c___ a fire / a problem / trouble	It's weird to see your own face in close-___ on TV.	She wanted to c___ the ant with her foot.	Gebet / p___
8	(to) give – (to) lend / (to) take – (to) b___	They also play the American n___ a___.	What did the girls discuss a___ themselves?	After high school, students can go to c___.	a___ tourists / visitors	She finally took pity ___ the dog and gave him her sausage.	Many people only p___ in church.	drücken / (to) s___

	Definitions	Verbs	Pictures	Context	The fourth word	German/English
1	a small, dirty area on your clothes: m _____	I always have tears in my eyes when I c _____ onions.		Our club's s _____ is: „We're the best in the west".	(to) explain – explanation (to) declare – d _____	War nur Spaß. J _____ k _____ .
2	a long journey by car: r _____ t _____	That was the doorbell. Can you a _____ the door, please?		At the age of ten he started playing in our j _____ football team.	2 days a week – part-time job 5 days a week – f _____ – _____ i _____	Erkenntnis, Einsicht r _____
3	work that you don't do the whole week: p _____ – _____ i _____	Oh it's you, Paul! I didn't r _____ you at first.		Are there other planets like the earth in the u _____ ?	internet – platform school – b _____ b _____	Was um alles in der Welt ...? W _____ e _____ ...?
4	low hills in front of higher mountains: f _____	Such animals do not e _____ in our country.	a _____ of paper	In the 1960s there were a _____ - segregation protests in New Orleans.	school – head teacher job – b _____	Nur zu, ihr drei. Y _____ t _____ g _____ a _____ .
5	almost blue: b _____	When I saw her reaction, I r _____ ed I had made a mistake.		A ship slowly appeared on the h _____ .	up – down forwards – b _____	Ich würde lieber ... I'd r _____ ...
6	A sweet drink popular in the US: s _____	I don't have a phone, but you can always c _____ me by email.		She finished her drink in one long s _____ .	long – whole story short – s _____	glamourös g _____
7	a part of a text, book, road, etc.: s _____	Behave yourself, Tom. Don't s _____ your tea like that.		He was a _____ to have a shower when the phone rang.	centre – central culture – c _____	glücklicherweise, zum Glück l _____
8	happening or done once every year: a _____	No tea for me. I p _____ coffee to tea.		Why do clocks actually t _____ ?	bag – thief house – b _____	Unabhängigkeit i _____

#	A wild ride	Verbs	Pictures	Context	Small words	German/English
1	Last week we went down the river in a r ____	If you can't see me, I will w ____ my hand.		There is a new and better v ____ of that program.	____ the time we arrived, he had already left.	Bundes- f ____
2	At first we didn't have to p ____ much.	It wasn't me! I s ____ I didn't steal the money!		I like watching films in the o ____ version.	Before she went out, she put ____ some lipstick.	Grillparty; Grill b ____
3	We just f ____ed down the peaceful river.	She's so funny. She always m ____s me laugh.		The sea was too r ____ to go out in a boat.	We didn't hit it ____ at first, but now we're best friends.	Kindheit c ____
4	Suddenly we became faster. We had hit w ____.	You can now t ____ your sheets over and start the test.		What I say officially is often not my p ____ opinion.	Don't do it tomorrow – do it right ____!	Bayern B ____
5	The water was really t ____ now.	s ____ c ____ of your father today. He's pretty angry with you!		Is that party a more formal or i ____ event?	Who's ____ for watching the football tonight?	Halt(et) mich auf dem Laufenden! k ____ p ____!
6	We had to steer through a narrow s ____ between the rocks.	Does that price i ____ tax?		3 October is a n ____ d ____ in Germany.	He ran all the way to school to arrive just ____ time for the lesson.	Sekretär/in s ____
7	Then we b ____ed against a rock and fell into the water.	Not everyone can join our club. We s ____ our members.		I like c ____ music, especially Mozart or Schubert.	Did the car flip ____ when it hit the tree?	(öffentlicher) Platz p ____
8	It was difficult to climb onto the o ____ raft.	When did America d ____ itself independent?		We have two TVs, but n ____ is working.	What type ____ person is your new teacher?	Chef/in b ____

The gerund as subject and object
Das Gerundium als Subjekt und als Objekt

▶ *pp. 18–21*

1 a) *Complete these sentences from 1 (pp. 18–19).*

Vervollständige diese Sätze aus 1 (S. 18–19).

Jasmine: "I love _____**ing**."

Tyler: "_____ here was a great idea, Jaz!"

Tyler suggested _____ Birdman.

Alex: "Pigeons are dirty! _____ them like that can make you sick!"

Alex: "You only play against these guys if you don't mind _____ your money."

b) *When an -ing form is used like a noun, it is called a **gerund**.*
*Look at these two sentences. Is the gerund the **subject** or the **object**? Tick the right box.*

*Wenn eine -ing-Form wie ein Nomen verwendet wird, dann wird sie **Gerundium** genannt.*
*Sieh dir diese zwei Sätze an. Ist das Gerundium das **Subjekt** oder das **Objekt**? Kreuze das richtige Kästchen an.*

Alex likes **playing chess**.

Chilling in Washington Square Park is fun.

☐ **subject** ☐ **object**

☐ **subject** ☐ **object**

2 a) *Some verbs are followed by a gerund, some are followed by an infinitive, and some are followed by a gerund or an infinitive. Look at the chart.*

Auf manche Verben folgt ein Gerundium, auf manche ein Infinitiv, und auf manche folgt ein Gerundium oder ein Infinitiv. Sieh dir die Tabelle an.

verb + gerund	verb + gerund or infinitive	verb + infinitive
enjoy, finish imagine, mind miss, practise suggest doing sth.	**begin/start continue, hate like, love, prefer** doing sth. *or* to do sth.	**would like would love would hate would prefer** to do sth.

b) *Gerund or to-infinitive? Complete the following sentences with the right form of the verb.*

Gerundium oder to-Infinitiv? Vervollständige die folgenden Sätze mit der richtigen Form des Verbs.

(live) Can you imagine _____ in New York?

(live) My grandparents would like _____ in the country.

(go – start) I don't mind _____ to school, but I'd prefer _____ a bit later.

(cook – wash) I enjoy _____, but I can't stand _____ the dishes.

3 *Now look at **Grammar File 1.1–1.2** on p. 171.*

*Schau dir jetzt **Grammar File 1.1–1.2** auf S. 171 an.*

English G Access | 4 Vocabulary & Language Action Sheets
Illustration: Tobias Dahmen, Utrecht
Niederlande, www.tobidahmen.de

The gerund after prepositions
Das Gerundium nach Präpositionen

▸ *pp. 18–21*

---

1 a) *Complete these sentences from 1 (pp. 18–19).*

Vervollständige diese Sätze aus 1 (S. 18–19).

Tyler wanted some good shots, but Alex was afraid of _____ too close.

Tyler: "You're good at chess. How about _____ with some of these guys?"

b) *Draw red boxes round the gerunds and blue boxes round the prepositions in front of them.*

Male rote Kästchen um die Gerundien und blaue Kästchen um die Präpositionen vor ihnen.

---

2 a) *Complete the following phrases with the correct prepositions. (You can check your answers on p. 172 of your English book.)*

Vervollständige die folgenden Ausdrücke mit den richtigen Präpositionen. (Du kannst deine Antworten auf S. 172 deines Englischbuchs überprüfen.)

(to) be **afraid** of____ doing sth.	the **chance** of____ doing sth.	(to) **believe** in____ doing sth.
(to) be **excited** _____ doing sth.	the **danger** _____ doing sth.	(to) **dream** _____ doing sth.
(to) be **good/bad** _____ doing sth.	the **idea** _____ doing sth.	(to) **talk** _____ doing sth.
(to) be **interested** ____ doing sth.	the **reason** _____ doing sth.	(to) **think** _____ doing sth.
(to) be **tired** _____ doing sth.	the **way** _____ doing sth.	(to) **worry** _____ doing sth.

b) *Write about yourself. There are some ideas in the box at the bottom. Use gerunds. And remember to use the correct preposition.*

Schreibe über dich selbst. Im Kästchen unten stehen ein paar Ideen. Verwende Gerundien. Und denk daran, die richtige Präposition zu verwenden.

I'm dreaming _____

I'm good _____

I'm bad _____

I'm worried _____

I'm keen _____

> tell jokes • visit Australia • play the guitar • skate • go to the dentist • change school •
> write poems • move to another town • surf • solve computer problems • give presentations • …

---

3 *Now look at **Grammar File 1.3** on pp. 172–173.*

*Schau dir jetzt **Grammar File 1.3** auf S. 172–173 an.*

English G Access | 4   Vocabulary & Language Action Sheets
Illustration: Tobias Dahmen, Utrecht
Niederlande, www.tobidahmen.de

REVISION   **Conditional sentences (types 1 and 2)**   ▶ *pp. 34–35, 37*
WIEDERHOLUNG **Bedingungssätze (Typ 1 und 2)**

1 a) *Complete these sentences from **1** (pp. 34–35).*   *Vervollständige diese Sätze aus **1** (S. 34–35).*

☐   You **wouldn't** _____ cold if you _____ here with me.

☐   It sounded awful. If he _____ that thing again, I**'ll** _____ crazy!

☐   If I ever _____ back, I'_____ straight for Bourbon Street.

☐   I _____ alligator if you _____ me a hundred bucks.

☐   If you _____ me one hundred dollars, I'_____ it again.

b) *Three of the conditional sentences in **1a** are* ***type 1**, two of them are **type 2**. Write "1" or "2" in the boxes in front of the sentences.*   *Drei der Bedingungssätze in **1a** sind vom **Typ 1**, zwei sind **Typ 2**. Schreibe „1" oder „2" in die Kästchen vor den Sätzen.*

c) *Which tenses are normally used in conditional sentences types 1 and 2? Complete:*   *Welche Zeiten werden normalerweise in Bedingungssätzen vom Typ 1 und 2 verwendet? Vervollständige:*

Type 1 *if*-clause: <u>simple</u> _____	main clause: _____
Type 2 *if*-clause: _____ _____	main clause: **w**_____ + _____

2 *Look at the sentences and complete the rule.*   *Sieh dir die Sätze an und vervollständige die Regel.*

If you like fast food, you can/could/should/must try our cheeseburger.

If we went to New Orleans, I could/might try gator on a stick.

Type 1: Instead of *will*, you can use _____ **in the main clause.**
Type 2: Instead of *would*, you can use _____ **in the main clause.**

3 *Who is fairly sure that the Walkers will **not** fly to the US in March? Tick the right box.*   *Wer ist ziemlich sicher, dass die Walkers im März **nicht** in die USA fliegen werden? Kreuze das richtige Kästchen an.*

Ava: *"If the Walkers **have** the money, they **will fly** to the US in March."*   ☐

Ella: *"If the Walkers **had** the money, they **would fly** to the US in March."*   ☐

4 *Now look at **Grammar File 2.1–2.2** on pp. 173–174.*   *Schau dir jetzt **Grammar File 2.1–2.2** auf S. 173–174 an.*

Cornelsen   English G Access | 4   Vocabulary & Language Action Sheets
Illustration: Tobias Dahmen, Utrecht
Niederlande, www.tobidahmen.de

Conditional sentences (type 3)   ▸ *pp. 40–43*
Bedingungssätze (Typ 3)

---

1 a) *Complete these sentences from **1** and **3** (pp. 40–41).*   *Vervollständige diese Sätze aus **1** und **3** (S. 40–41).*

"I mean, you **wouldn't** _____ the earrings if you _____ liked him."

Life for their children _____ _____ _____ very different if they _____ _____
up the fight.

b) *Underline the if-clauses in **1a** with a green pen and the main clauses with a red pen. Then complete the rule:*   *Unterstreiche die if-Sätze in **1a** mit einem grünen Stift und die Hauptsätze mit einem roten Stift. Dann vervollständige die Regel.*

> **Type 3**
>
> **if**-clause: p_____ p_____   main clause: w_____ + _____ + **past pa**_____

---

2 a) *Read these sentences. Underline the correct verb forms. Cross out the wrong verb forms.*   *Lies die folgenden Sätze. Unterstreiche die richtigen Verbformen. Streiche die falschen Verbformen durch.*

(1) If it hadn't rained, they **had gone** / **would have gone** swimming.

(2) His father would have been angry if he **had dropped** / **would have dropped** the glasses.

b) *Look again at your sentences from **2a**. What is correct for sentence (1), what is correct for sentence (2)? Tick the right boxes.*   *Sieh dir deine Sätze in **2a** noch einmal an. Was ist korrekt für Satz (1), was ist korrekt für Satz (2)? Kreuze die richtigen Kästchen an.*

(1) It rained, so they didn't go swimming.   ☐

     It didn't rain, so they went swimming.   ☐

(2) His father was angry because he dropped the glasses.   ☐

     He didn't drop the glasses so his father wasn't angry.   ☐

---

3 *Read sentence (1a). Then complete the conditional sentence (1b).*   *Lies den Satz (1a). Dann vervollständige den Bedingungssatz (1b).*

(1a) It was nice and warm that day, so we had a barbecue in the garden.

(1b) If it **hadn't** _____ that day we _____
     a barbecue in the garden.

---

4 *Now look at **Grammar file 2.3** on pp. 174–175.*      *Schau dir jetzt **Grammar file 2.3** auf S. 174–175 an.*

English G Access | 4 Vocabulary & Language Action Sheets
Illustration: Tobias Dahmen, Utrecht
Niederlande, www.tobidahmen.de

Countable and uncountable nouns
Zählbare und nicht zählbare Nomen   ▶ *pp. 46–47*

---

1 a) *Complete these sentences from 1 (p. 46).*   *Vervollständige diese Sätze aus 1 (S. 46).*

Tyler had never seen so much _____: there were large oval **plates** … and a huge _____.

The **porch** was right on the _____.

And here's some _____ – make sure he's dead before you pull him into your _____.

"I say it's _____ for a little _____!" Eugene took a _____ from his **pocket** and played a

few _____.

b) *All the words you needed to complete the*   *Alle Wörter, die du brauchtest, um die Sätze in **1a** zu*
*sentences in **1a** are nouns. Five of them are*   *vervollständigen, sind Nomen. Fünf von ihnen sind*
uncountable. *Draw a red box round the*   **nicht zählbar**. *Male ein rotes Kästchen um die **nicht***
uncountable *nouns.*   **zählbaren** *Nomen.*

c) *There are four **quantifiers** in the sentences*   *Es gibt vier **Mengenangaben** in den Sätzen in **1a**.*
*in **1a**. Mark them with a highlighter.*   *Markiere sie mit einem Textmarker.*

d) *Now complete the chart below with the*   *Vervollständige nun die Tabelle unten mit den **Mengen-***
quantifiers *from the box.*   **angaben** *aus dem Kästchen.*

> some • many • much • a lot of • a little • a few

quantifier + plural of countable noun	quantifier + uncountable noun
_____	_____
_____ ⟨ plates, turkeys, notes …	_____ ⟨ food, water, advice, information, money, experience, …
_____	_____

---

2 *Please translate. Use **a lot of, a few, a little**.*   *Bitte übersetze. Verwende **a lot of, a few, a little**.*

viele Möbel _____   viele Hausaufgaben _____

ein paar Stühle _____   viel Musik _____

etwas Milch _____   einige Übungen _____

ein paar Gläser _____   ein bisschen Geld _____

---

3 *Now look at **Grammar file 4***   *Schau dir jetzt **Grammar file 4** auf S. 176–177 an.*
on pp. 176–177.

English G Access | 4 Vocabulary & Language Action Sheets
Illustration: Tobias Dahmen, Utrecht
Niederlande, www.tobidahmen.de

The passive: different tenses
Das Passiv: verschiedene Zeiten   ▶ *pp. 56, 58*

---

1 a) **REVISION** *Complete these sentences from* ***1*** *(p. 56).*   *Vervollständige diese Sätze aus* ***1*** *(S. 56).*

"The bathroom wasn't great. I'm sure it _____ n't _____ before we moved in."

"I'm really sorry …," Hailey began, but she ____ _____ by the woman.

b) *Now find these sentences in* ***1*** *(p. 56) and complete them.*   *Nun finde diese Sätze in* ***1*** *(S. 56) und vervollständige sie.*

"Seals can get very angry. People _____ _____ bitten, you know."

"I___ ____ _____ to L.A. next weekend – to interview Brandon Williams."

---

2 *Complete the chart.*   *Vervollständige die Tabelle.*

The passive

simple present	am/are/is + past _____
	Example: The bathrooms **are** _____ (clean) every morning.
simple past	_____
	Example: In 2011, the hotel _____ (destroy) in a fire.
present perfect	_____
	Example: These windows _____ (not clean) for years.

---

3 *Read these sentences. Underline the correct verb forms. Cross out the wrong verb forms.*   *Lies die folgenden Sätze. Unterstreiche die richtigen Verbformen. Streiche die falschen Verbformen durch.*

Thousands of visitors **have been welcomed** / **have welcomed** at Moss Beach since it **was made** / **were made** a state reserve in 1969.

The marine reserve **supports** / **is supported** by volunteers from all over the US.

Someone **was bitten** / **was biting** by a seal last Sunday.

---

4 *Now look at* ***Grammar file 5.1–5.2*** *(p. 178).*

Schau dir jetzt ***Grammar file 5.1–5.2*** *(S. 178).*

English G Access | 4   Vocabulary & Language Action Sheets
Illustration: Tobias Dahmen, Utrecht
Niederlande, www.tobidahmen.de

The passive of verbs with two objects

Das Passiv von Verben mit zwei Objekten

▶ *pp. 60–62*

---

1 a) *Look at these two **active** sentences:*

(1) Three months later they **offered** him the role.

(2) They **gave** him one week to learn his lines.

The sentences each have an indirect object ('person object') and a direct object ('thing object'). Underline the objects with two different colours.

b) *Now complete these two **passive** sentences from p. 61 and translate them.*

(3) Brandon: "Three months later ___ **was** _____ the role."

„Drei Monate später wurde _____."

(4) Brandon: "I _____ just one week to learn all my lines."

„_____, meinen gesamten Text zu lernen."

c) *Look at this German sentence. How would you say that in English? Cross out the wrong sentence. (You can find the correct English sentence on p. 60.)*

Ihr werden eine Menge Fragen gestellt … .

*Sieh dir diese beiden **Aktiv**sätze an:*

(1) Drei Monate später boten sie ihm die Rolle an.

(2) Sie gaben ihm eine Woche, seinen Text zu lernen.

Die Sätze haben jeweils ein indirektes Objekt („Personenobjekt") und ein direktes Objekt („Sachobjekt"). Unterstreiche die Objekte mit zwei verschiedenen Farben.

*Nun vervollständige diese beiden **Passiv**sätze von S. 61 und übersetze sie.*

Sieh dir diesen deutschen Satz an. Wie würdest du das auf Englisch sagen? Streiche den falschen Satz durch. (Du kannst den richtigen englischen Satz auf S. 60 finden.)

a) **She** is asked lots of questions … .
b) **Her** is asked lots of questions … .

---

2 *Make **passive** sentences (in the simple past).*

*Bilde **Passiv**sätze (im simple past).*

(She / offer / a menu) _____

(They / pay / a lot of money for the job) _____

(He / promise / a TV role) _____

---

3 *Now look at **Grammar file 5.3** on pp. 179–180.*

*Schau dir jetzt **Grammar file 5.3** auf S. 179–180 an.*

English G Access | 4 Vocabulary & Language Action Sheets
Illustration: Tobias Dahmen, Utrecht
Niederlande, www.tobidahmen.de

The *to*-infinitive
Der Infinitiv mit *to*

▶ *pp. 56, 58*

---

1 a) *Complete the sentence from 1 (p. 56). Then complete the translation too.*

Vervollständige den Satz aus 1 (S. 56). Dann vervollständige auch die Übersetzung.

Mrs Miller: "So _____ with your father."

„Daher **möchte ich,** _____ **mitfährst.**"

b) *Look at this German sentence. How would you say that in English? Cross out the wrong sentence. (You can find the correct English sentence on p. 181.)*

Sieh dir diesen deutschen Satz an. Wie würdest du das auf Englisch sagen? Streiche den falschen Satz durch. (Du kannst den richtigen englischen Satz auf S. 181 finden.)

Haileys Mutter wollte, dass Hailey mit ihrem Vater mitfährt.

a)   Hailey's mother wanted Hailey to go with her father.

b)   Hailey's mother wanted that Hailey went with her father.

---

2 *Now complete and translate these sentences.*

Vervollständige und übersetze jetzt diese Sätze.

(expect – me – be home)   My parents _____ **to be home** by 9 pm.

Meine Eltern erwarten,_____.

(told – her – wait outside)   The policewoman _____.

Die Polizistin_____.

(wanted – us – sing along)   The singer _____ with him.

Der Sänger _____.

---

3 REVISION *Complete and translate these sentences.*

Wiederholung *Vervollständige und übersetze diese Sätze.*

(how / install this program)   Can you show me _____ **this program**?

Kannst du mir zeigen, _____.

(where / put her dirty boots)   She asked me _____.

Sie fragte mich, _____.

---

4 *Now look at **Grammar file 6** on pp. 180–181.*

*Schau dir jetzt **Grammar file 6** auf S. 180–181 an.*

English G Access | 4   Vocabulary & Language Action Sheets
Illustration: Tobias Dahmen, Utrecht
Niederlande, www.tobidahmen.de

REVISION　　**Indirect speech: statements**　　　　　▶ *p. 76*
WIEDERHOLUNG　　Die indirekte Rede: Aussagesätze

---

1 a) *Look at the sentences and complete them. (You can check the indirect speech on p. 76.)*　　*Sieh dir die Sätze an und vervollständige sie. (Du kannst die indirekte Rede auf S. 76 überprüfen.)*

direct speech	indirect speech
(1) Coach: "Your times are really good."	Coach **told** me my times _____ really good.
(2) Coach: "You are too slow."	He **said** I _____ too slow.
(3) Dad: "You can use it while I'm gone."	Dad **said** I _____ use it while he **was** gone.

b) *If you report what someone **said**, the verb forms usually move back one step into the past ('backshift of tenses'). Complete the chart.*　　*Wenn man berichtet, was jemand **gesagt hat**, dann verschieben sich in der Regel die Zeitformen um eine Stufe in die Vergangenheit. Vervollständige die Tabelle.*

present	▶ past	"You are"	▶ … said I _____	
can	▶ _____	"You can"	▶ … said I _____	
past	▶ p_____ p_____	"You went"	▶ … said I **had** _____	
present perfect	▶ p_____ p_____	"You've done"	▶ … said I **had** _____	
***will*-future**	▶ w_____ + infinitive	"You'll see"	▶ … said I _____ + **see**	

---

2 *Report what these people said.*　　*Berichte, was diese Leute gesagt haben.*

(1) Drew: "It's Dad's truck."

Drew **said** that _____

(2) Drew: "Hey! Kaya! I watched you during practice."

Drew **told** Kaya that he _____ **her during practice.**

(3) Kaya: "I don't have a car."

Kaya **told** Drew that _____

(4) Drew: "I can drive you."

Drew **answered** that _____

---

3 *Now look at **Grammar file 8.1** on p. 183.*

*Schau dir jetzt **Grammar file 8.1** auf S. 183 an.*

English G Access | 4　Vocabulary & Language Action Sheets
Illustration: Tobias Dahmen, Utrecht
Niederlande, www.tobidahmen.de

Indirect speech: questions
Die indirekte Rede: Fragen

▶ *pp. 82–85*

---

1 a) *Find these sentences in the second half of **1** (p. 82) and complete them.*

*Finde diese Sätze in der zweiten Hälfte von **1** (S. 82) und vervollständige sie.*

(1) I **asked** him _____ I _____ make the team.

(2) He **asked** _____ mom and I _____ in Mobridge.

(3) He **asked** me _____ I _____ on the weekend.

(4) He **asked** _____ I _____ to Mount Rushmore with him.

b) *What did they say in direct speech? (Look at the first half of p. 82 if you need help.)*

Was haben sie in direkter Rede gesagt? (Schau in der ersten Hälfte von S. 82 nach, wenn du Hilfe brauchst.)

(1) Kaya: " I _____ make the team?"

(2) Cody: "_____ you and your mom _____ in Mobridge?"

(3) Drew: "_____ you _____ on the weekend?"

(4) Drew: "_____ you **come** with us?"

---

2 *Complete the following four examples. Then complete the rules below.*

Vervollständige die folgenden vier Beispiele. Dann vervollständige die Regeln darunter.

wh-questions "Where's Kaya?" ▶ He asked _____ Kaya was.

"When do you usually have dinner?" ▶ She asked _____ we usually had dinner.

Yes/No questions "Are you OK?" ▶ She wanted to know ____ (*or:* _____) I was OK.

"Do you like cats?" ▶ He wanted to know ____ (*or:* _____) I liked cats.

– When you report **wh-questions**, you use the _____ from the direct question.

– When you report **yes/no questions**, you need ____ or _____.

---

3 *Report what Jodi wanted to know.*

Berichte, was Jodi wissen wollte.

Jodi: "How long have you known him, Kaya?"

Jodi **wanted to know** how long Kaya _____ Drew.

---

4 *Now look at **Grammar file 8.2** on p. 184.*

*Schau dir jetzt **Grammar file 8.2** auf S. 184 an.*

English G Access | 4 Vocabulary & Language Action Sheets
Illustration: Tobias Dahmen, Utrecht
Niederlande, www.tobidahmen.de

Indirect speech: commands, requests, advice, suggestions   ▸ *pp. 88, 90*
Die indirekte Rede: Aufforderungen, Bitten, Ratschläge, Vorschläge

---

1 *Complete these sentences from 1 (p. 88) and the rules below.*   *Vervollständige diese Sätze aus **1** (S. 88) und die Regeln darunter.*

(1) Kaya: "My Aunt Jodi says Mount Rushmore is an insult to the Lakota people.

   She _____ me _____ there."

(2) Drew: "I asked_____ because I thought it would be fun."

– When you report **commands** (e.g. "Don't go there."), you use _____ sb. to do sth.

– When you report **requests** (e.g. "Can you come with us?"), you use _____

---

2 *Look at what Coach said to Kaya one day:*   *Sieh dir an, was Coach eines Tages zu Kaya sagte:*

Coach: "You should try to speed up a bit if you want to qualify, Kaya."

*Report what he said. Use the verb **advise**:*   *Berichte, was er gesagt hat. Verwende das Verb **advise**:*

Coach _____ Kaya _____ if she wanted to qualify.

Now complete the rule.   *Jetzt vervollständige die Regel.*

– When you report **advice**, you use _____ sb. to do sth.

---

3 *Complete this sentence from 1 (p. 88).*   *Vervollständige diesen Satz aus **1** (S. 88).*

Bobby came up and _____ for a pizza.

This is what Bobby said to Drew. Complete it.   *Dies hat Bobby zu Drew gesagt. Vervollständige es.*

Bobby: "Hey Drew, _____ for a pizza."

*How can you report what someone **suggested**? Here are four alternatives – **three are correct, one is wrong**.*   *Wie kann man berichten, was jemand **vorgeschlagen** hat? Hier sind vier Alternativen – **drei sind richtig, eine ist falsch**.*

> **When you want to report suggestions, you can use …**

- [ ] **a** X suggested doing sth.
- [ ] **b** X suggested that I/we do sth.
- [ ] **c** X suggested to do sth.
- [ ] **d** X suggested I/we should do sth.

---

4 *Now look at **Grammar file 8.3** on pp. 184–185.*      *Schau dir jetzt **Grammar file 8.3** auf S. 184–185 an.*

English G Access | 4   Vocabulary & Language Action Sheets
Illustration: Tobias Dahmen, Utrecht
Niederlande, www.tobidahmen.de

The definite article
Der bestimmte Artikel

▶ *pp. 83, 86*

---

1 a) *Compare these sentence pairs:*   *Vergleiche diese Satzpaare:*

In the 1960s, **life** began to improve for the Lakota.   Horses are important in **the life** of the Lakota.

We can learn a lot from **history**.   Through storytellers, Native American children learned **the history** of their communities.

Sport is healthy, and **sport** can be fun.   But **the sport** we did at school was boring.

You need **oil** if you want to fry potatoes in a frying pan.   **The oil** that they used for the chips was old and smelled disgusting.

Kids usually like ice cream.   Have you heard about **the kids** who saved a baby whale?

b) *Tick the right box:*   *Kreuze das richtige Kästchen an:*

– Nouns used in a **general sense** are used   ☐ with the definite article

☐ without the definite article.

– Nouns used in a **specific sense** are used   ☐ with the definite article

☐ without the definite article.

---

2 a) *Now compare these sentence pairs:*   *Jetzt vergleiche diese Satzpaare:*

A boy got hurt and was taken to **hospital**.   We live right next to **the hospital**.

We always go to **church** on Sundays.   Don't miss the concert in **the church**.

Let's go for an ice cream after **school**.   Let's meet behind **the school** as usual.

Some of the protesters were sent to **prison**.   He works in the factory behind **the prison**.

b) *Complete the rule:*   *Vervollständige die Regel:*

The nouns *church, hospital, prison, school, college, university* are used …

– _____ **the definite article** when we are talking about the **purpose ("Zweck") of the building**.

– _____ **the definite article** when we are talking about the **building itself**.

---

3 *Now look at **Grammar file 10** on pp. 186–187.*   *Schau dir jetzt **Grammar file 10** auf S. 186–187 an.*

REVISION   **Relative clauses**   ▸ *pp. 96–97, 108–110*
WIEDERHOLUNG **Relativsätze**

---

1 a) *Look at these sentences:*   *Sieh dir diese Sätze an:*

A woman **who** was wearing high heels answered the door.

Two teenagers **that** were carrying big suitcases walked up behind Dan and David.

Where are the pictures of Hailey and Tyler **which** were lying on my desk?

He washed off the marks **that** her lipstick had left on his shirt.

b) *Complete the rule.*   *Vervollständige die Regel.*

You use • _____ **for people**	• _____ **for things**	• _____ **for people and things**

---

2 *"who"-words or "which"-words? Write the*   *"who"-Wörter oder "which"-Wörter? Schreib die*
nouns from the box in the right group.   *Nomen aus dem Kasten in die richtige Gruppe.*

banjo • city • guard • magazine • national park • people • person • protests • stranger • teenager • visitors • whale

"who"-words: guard, _____

"which"-words: banjo, _____

---

3 a) *One of the following four sentences is* **wrong.**   *Einer der vier folgenden Sätze ist falsch. Welcher?*
Which one? Cross it out.   *Streiche ihn durch.*

(1) "Here's a photo **that** shows me and your grandma at the concert."

(2) "Here's a photo shows me and your grandma at the concert."

(3) "What's that big announcement **that** Mark is going to make?"

(4) "What's that big announcement Mark is going to make?"

b) *Can you complete the rules now?*   *Kannst du jetzt die Regeln vervollständigen?*

When the relative pronoun is the _____ of the relative clause as in sentence _____,
you can leave it out. A relative clause without a relative pronoun is called "contact clause".

When the relative pronoun is the _____ of the relative clause as in sentence _____,
you mustn't leave it out.

---

4 *Now look at* **Grammar file 13**      *Schau dir jetzt* **Grammar file 13** *auf S. 190–192 an.*
on pp. 190–192.

English G Access | 4 Vocabulary & Language Action Sheets
Illustration: Tobias Dahmen, Utrecht
Niederlande, www.tobidahmen.de

The present participle (I)
Das Partizip Präsens (I)

▸ *pp. 96–97*

---

1 a) *Complete the sentences from 1 (p. 96).*   *Vervollständige die Sätze aus **1** (S. 96).*

When I rang the bell, a woman _____ **high heels** answered the door.

Two teenagers _____ **big suitcases** walked up behind them.

b) *Rephrase the sentences from **1a**.*   *Schreibe die Sätze aus **1a** um. Verwende **who** ... .*
*Use **who** ... .*

When I rang the bell, a woman _____ answered the door.

Two teenagers _____ walked up behind them.

---

2 *Here are four statements about **participle clauses** – three are correct, one is wrong. Tick the correct ones, cross out the wrong one.*   *Hier sind vier Aussagen über **Partizipialsätze** – drei sind richtig, eine ist falsch. Kreuz die richtigen an, streiche die falsche durch.*

> **Participle clauses**
> **(e. g. a woman *wearing high heels*) ...**

- [ ] **a** come directly after a noun.
- [ ] **b** contain *who*, *which* or *that*.
- [ ] **c** can tell us what is or was happening.
- [ ] **d** can be used instead of a relative clause.

---

3 *Complete these sentences. Use participle clauses.*   *Vervollständige diese Sätze. Verwende Partizipialsätze.*

Do you know the **boy playing** _____?
(he's playing the guitar)

The dogs _____ are really cute.
(they're fighting over the ball)

Whose are all the **shoes** _____?
(they're lying around in the living room)

The photo shows a **woman** _____.
(she's entering a bank)

They picked up the **rubbish** _____.
(it was lying on the ground)

---

4 *Now look at **Grammar file 12.1 and 12.2** on p. 189.*      *Schau dir jetzt **Grammar file 12.1 und 12.2** auf S. 189 an.*

English G Access | 4   Vocabulary & Language Action Sheets
Illustration: Tobias Dahmen, Utrecht
Niederlande, www.tobidahmen.de

The present participle (II)   ▶ *pp. 103–104*
Das Partizip Präsens (II)

1 a) *Complete the sentences from 3 (p. 103).*   *Vervollständige die Sätze aus 3 (S. 103).*

We watched a family of beavers _____ in the river.

And Tyler _____ a mule deer _____ a drink.

I _____ tightening on the paddle.

I heard _____ our names.

Then I _____ Julie _____ onto the overturned raft.

b) *Draw red boxes round the verbs and blue*   *Male rote Kästchen um die Verben und blaue Kästchen*
boxes round the present participles.   *um die present participles.*
Then complete the rule: *Dann vervollständige die Regel:*

> **If you want to say that you feel, hear, notice, see, … something that is (or was) going on,**
>
> **you can use a verb of perception + o_____ + p_____ p_____ .**

2 *Look at the verbs in the box. Which of them are*   *Sieh dir die Verben im Kasten an. Welche von ihnen*
***verbs of perception**? Mark them in yellow.*   *sind Verben der Wahrnehmung? Markiere sie gelb.*

> (to) **ask** • (to) **feel** • (to) **finish** • (to) **gaze** • (to) **hear** • (to) **help** • (to) **listen to** • (to) **look at** •
> (to) **miss** • (to) **notice** • (to) **see** • (to) **shout** • (to) **smell** • (to) **spend** • (to) **spot** • (to) **watch**

3 *Complete these sentences. Use participle*   *Vervollständige diese Sätze. Verwende Partizipialsätze.*
clauses.

(hear/bark)   There are a couple of dogs outside. I can _____ them barking.

(smell/burn)   Can you _____ something _____? Is there a fire?

(hear/ring)   Can you _____ our neighbour's phone _____? It makes me want to scream.

(notice/shout) When we walked past the football pitch, we _____ a man _____
                    at some kids.

4 *Now look at **Grammar file 12.3***      *Schau dir jetzt **Grammar file 12.3** auf S. 189–190 an.*
on pp. 189–190.

Vocabulary Action Sheets – Lösungen

	Big cities	Verbs	Pictures	German/English	American English words	Context
1	boroughs	roar	statue	shot	apartment	central
2	subway	arrest	lockers	man-made	cookie	Liberty
3	square	lean	railing	awesome	garbage	metal
4	blocks	crash	newspaper	inch	line	backpack
5	storeys (BE) / stories (AE)	collapse	rose	I'd (I had) better	pants	used to
6	elevators	mind	cemetery	I guess	sidewalk	feet
7	avenues	click	observation deck	weirdo	store	indoor
8	suburb	bake	pigeon	suggestion	vacation	difference

Unit 1.1

	American spelling	Verbs	Pictures	German/English	Small words	Context
1	center	program	tracks	guy	out	insulted
2	color	take	factory	legendary	of	pressure
3	traveled	bloom	turkey	Ladies and gentlemen	to	move
4	meter	assess	roller coaster	timer	on	stand
5	favorite	divide	shrub	whose	down	railway (BE) / railroad (AE)
6	traveling	refer	lawn	seed	of	frozen
7	theater	make	sheet	council	on	performance
8	neighbor	keep	diagram	delivery	up	limit

Unit 1.2

	Adjectives	Cooking	Context	Definitions	Verbs	Pictures	American English	German/ English
1	crazy	dish	hurricane	swamp	freeze	brass band	movie theater	Mardi Gras
2	disgusting	ingredients	colony	kinda	combine	alligator	closet	both ... and ...
3	public	boils	degrees	Native Americans	fry	palm tree	jewelry	Why not try ...?
4	allergic	saucepan	Celsius	beef	roast	sausages	downtown	I would have screamed too.
5	sharp	frying pan	straight	great-grandfather	recommend	shrimp	restroom	honey
6	impatient	oven	settlers	native speaker	fancy	chicken	diner	He had killed it himself.
7	strict	cook	occasions	cotton	tune	waiter/ waitress	streetcar	all over the city
8	tiny	sauce	tinned	centimetres	tighten	string	elevator	pattern

Unit 2.1

Vocabulary Action Sheets – Lösungen

	The fourth word	Food	Context	Blacks in America	Verbs	Pictures	Writing a text	German/English
1	buck	stew	powder	In the 1960s	belong	porch	style	cranberry
2	tradition	herb	typical	segregation	beat up	pile	synonym	mind
3	pork	spice	wedding	prejudices	murder	counter	relevant	a little
4	dairy products	sour	real	discrimination	speak out	pumpkin	paraphrase	limited
5	menu	bitter	round	called names	hunt	line	skim	leather
6	light	hot	advice	courage	flashed	hook	heading	medium
7	oval	spicy	permission	civil rights	shoot	harmonica	sub-headings	wildlife
8	Fahrenheit	pie	square	generation	rebuild	triangular	graphics	documentary

Unit 2.2

	A wildfire	Pictures	Context	Opposites	Definitions	Verbs	German/English
1	reserve	desert	completely	uncomfortable	image	stretch	the week before
2	emergency	skyscrapers	contrast	(to) give	foreign	spot	Sorry?
3	residents	parking lot / car park	marine	separately	stranger	look out	I'd like you to help me.
4	unstoppable	shell	social	illegal	hostess	support	saying
5	fire department	sunset	at all	(to) prevent	noon	reveal	ecology
6	burnt	trash can / rubbish bin	common	effect	environment	tutors	I'm feeling faint.
7	cause	fumes	reaction	safe	expert	set up	although
8	droughts	ID	process	possible	permit	switch	quote/quotation

Unit 3.1

	Hollywood	Pictures	Context	Adjectives	The fourth word	Verbs	German/English
1	celebrities	wildfire	change	cute	line	pat	discovery
2	VIP	limousine	stay	dignified	pronounce	go viral	the latest
3	security	receptionist	atmosphere	optimistic	season	discover	Stay posted.
4	take	microphone	Ms / Ms.	shiny	explanation	evacuate	miles per hour (mph)
5	script	flame	power	powerful	(to) flow	have	My heart goes out to …
6	season	campfire	cut off	emotional	tenth grade	investigate	prefix
7	programs	firefighter	climate	neutral	landscape	compare	outline
8	Channel	helicopter	opposite	catchy	relaxed	experience	briefly

Unit 3.2

Vocabulary Action Sheets – Lösungen

	Adjectives	South Dakota	Context	Definitions	Verbs	Pictures	American English	German/ English
1	dusty	Badlands	somewhere	footstep	slap	sculpture	counter(top)	No wonder
2	excellent	prairie	extra	mood	honk	engine	water fountain	talking
3	glum	reservations	property	technique	tucked	track	period	it takes practice
4	sacred	tribes	law	bilingual	advise	(steering) wheel	grade	whether
5	heartless	Conflict	choice	messenger	speed up	buffalo	driver's license	in recent years
6	offensive	cloudless	insult	(to) return	qualify	graffiti	principal	anyway
7	wonderful	rodeo	giant	weekday	notice	floodlights	percent	for this reason
8	filthy	gallop	tax	storytelling	came up	dam	ride	even though

Unit 4.1

	The fourth word	Mount Rushmore	Context	School in the USA	Verb phrases	Small words	Verbs	German/ English
1	silence	granite	service	register	lend	for	pass	not (...) any longer
2	coach	carve	hardly	literature	crown	into	forced	more than in any other place
3	(to) fail	taxpayers'	part	social studies	take care of	on	changed	fairly
4	support	relations	relationship	assignments	introduce	of	spray	however
5	at any time	extremely	engine	attend	govern	to	gazes	long shot
6	continent	patriotism	surprising	sessions	move	in	keep up	medium shot
7	strength	ceremony	moral	grounds	cause	up	crush	prayer
8	(to) borrow	national anthem	among	college	attract	on	pray	(to) squeeze

Unit 4.2

	Definitions	Verbs	Pictures	Context	The fourth word	German/English
1	mark	chop	high heels	slogan	declaration	Just kidding
2	road trip	answer	lipstick	junior	full-time job	realization
3	part-time job	recognize	suitcase	universe	bulletin board	What on earth ...?
4	foothills	exist	stack	anti-	boss	You three go ahead.
5	blu(e)ish	realized	raft	horizon	backwards	I'd rather ...
6	soda	contact	apron	slurp	summary	glamorous
7	section	slurp	paddle	was about to	cultural	luckily
8	annual	prefer	beaver	tick	burglar	independence

Unit 5.1

Vocabulary Action Sheets – Lösungen

	A wild ride	Verbs	Pictures	Context	Small words	German/English
1	raft	wave	bull	version	By	federal
2	paddle	swear	balloon	original	on	barbecue
3	floated	makes	pier	rough	off	childhood
4	whitewater	turn	trap	personal	away	Bavaria
5	turbulent	Steer clear	squirrel	informal	up	Keep me posted!
6	space	include	crutch	national day	in	secretary
7	bumped	select	scales	classical	over	plaza
8	overturned	declare	kettle	neither	of	boss

Unit 5.2

LAS 1.1

1 a) Jasmine: "I love **drawing**."
Tyler: "**Coming** here was a great idea, Jaz!"
Tyler suggested **visiting** Birdman.
Alex: "Pigeons are dirty! **Touching** them like that can make you sick!"
Alex: "You only play against these guys if you don't mind **losing** your money."

b) Alex likes **playing chess**. **object**
Chilling in Washington Square Park is fun. **subject**

2 b) Can you imagine **living** in New York?
My grandparents would like **to live** in the country.
I don't mind **going** to school, but I'd prefer **to start** a bit later.
I enjoy **cooking**, but I can't stand **washing** the dishes.

LAS 1.2

1 a) Tyler wanted some good shots, but Alex was afraid **of getting** too close.
Tyler: "You're good at chess. How **about playing** with some of these guys?"

2 a)
(to) be **afraid of** doing sth.	the **chance of** doing sth.	(to) **believe in** doing sth.
(to) be **excited about** doing sth.	the **danger of** doing sth.	(to) **dream of/about** doing sth.
(to) be **good/bad at** doing sth.	the **idea of** doing sth.	(to) **talk about/of** doing sth.
(to) be **interested in** doing sth.	the **reason for** doing sth.	(to) **think of** doing sth.
(to) be **tired of** doing sth.	the **way of** doing sth.	(to) **worry about** doing sth.

b) I'm **dreaming of** visiting Australia/…
I'm **good at** telling jokes/…
I'm **bad at** surfing/…
I'm **worried about** giving presentations/…
I'm **keen on** playing the guitar/…

LAS 2.1

1 a, b) 2 You **wouldn't be** cold if you **were** here with me.
1 It sounded awful. If he **plays** that thing again, **I'll go** crazy!
1 If I ever **come** back, **I'll head** straight for Bourbon Street.
2 I **wouldn't eat** alligator if you **gave** me a hundred bucks.
1 If you **give** me one hundred dollars, **I'll eat** it again.

1 c) Type 1 **if**-clause: **simple present** main clause: **will-future**
Type 2 **if**-clause: **simple past** main clause: **would** + **infinitive**

2 Type 1 Instead of *will*, you can use **can, could, should or must** in the main clause.
Type 2 Instead of *would*, you can use **could or might** in the main clause.

3 **Ella** is fairly sure that the Walkers will <u>not</u> fly to the US in March.

LAS 2.2

1 a) "I mean, you **wouldn't have kept** the earrings if you **hadn't liked** him."
Life for their children **would have been** very different if they **had given** up the fight.

b) Type 3   *if*-clause: past perfect   main clause: *would + have* + past participle

2 a) (1) If it hadn't rained, they **would have gone** swimming.
(2) His father would have been angry if he **had dropped** the glasses.

b) (1) It rained, so they didn't go swimming.
(2) He didn't drop the glasses so his father wasn't angry.

3   If it **hadn't been nice and warm** that day we **wouldn't have had** a barbecue in the garden

---

LAS 2.3

1 a) Tyler had never seen so much **food**: there were large oval **plates** … and a huge **turkey**.
The **porch** was right on the **water**.
And here's some **advice** – make sure he's dead before you pull him into your **boat**.
"I say it's **time** for a little **music**!" Eugene took a **harmonica** from his **pocket** and played a few **notes**.

b) uncountable: **food; water; advice; time; music**

c) quantifiers: **much; some; a little; a few**

d) quantifier + plural of countable noun: <u>**some / many / a lot of / a few**</u>   **plates, turkeys, notes, …**
quantifier + uncountable noun: <u>**some / much / a lot of / a little**</u>   **food, water, advice, information, money, experience, …**

2

viele Möbel	**a lot of furniture**	viele Hausaufgaben	**a lot of homework**
ein paar Stühle	**a few chairs**	viel Musik	**a lot of music**
etwas Milch	**a little milk**	einige Übungen	**a few exercises**
ein paar Gläser	**a few glasses**	ein bisschen Geld	**a little money**

LAS 3.1

1 a) "The bathroom wasn't great. I'm sure it **wasn't cleaned** before we moved in."
"I'm really sorry …," Hailey began, but she **was interrupted** by the woman.

b) "Seals can get very angry. People **have been bitten**, you know."
"**I've been invited** to L.A. next weekend – to interview Brandon Williams."

2   **The passive**

simple present	am/are/is + past participle	(The bathrooms **are cleaned** every morning.)
simple past	was/were + past participle	(In 2011, the hotel **was destroyed** in a fire.)
present perfect	have/has been + past participle	(These windows **haven't been cleaned** for years.)

3   Thousands of visitors **have been welcomed** at Moss Beach since it **was made** a state reserve in 1969.
The marine reserve **is supported** by volunteers from all over the US.
Someone **was bitten** by a seal last Sunday.

LAS 3.2

1 a) (1) Three months later they offered him the role.
   indirect object ('person object'): him *(ihm)*   **direct object ('thing object'): the role *(die Rolle)***
   (2) They gave him one week to learn his lines.
   indirect object ('person object'): him *(ihm)*   **direct object ('thing object'): one week *(eine Woche)***

  b) (3) Brandon: "Three months later **I was offered** the role."
   „Drei Monate später **wurde mir die Rolle angeboten**."
   (4) Brandon :   "**I was given** just one week to learn all my lines."
   „**Mir wurde nur eine Woche gegeben**, meinen gesamten Text zu lernen."

  c) **Ihr** werden eine Menge Fragen gestellt … .   **She** is asked lots of questions … .

2   **She was offered a menu.**
     They were paid a lot of money for the job.
     He was promised a TV role.

LAS 3.3

1 a) Mrs Miller: "So **I'd like you to go** with your father."
   „Daher **möchte ich, dass du mit deinem Vater mitfährst**."

  b) Haileys Mutter wollte, dass Hailey mit ihrem Vater mitfährt.
   Hailey's mother **wanted Hailey to go** with her father.

2   My parents **expect me to be home** by 9 pm.
     Meine Eltern erwarten, **dass ich bis 9 Uhr / um 9 Uhr zu Hause bin**.

     The policewoman **told her to wait outside**.
     Die Polizistin **sagte ihr, dass sie draußen warten sollte / forderte sie auf, draußen zu warten**.

     The singer **wanted us to sing along** with him.
     Der Sänger **wollte, dass wir mitsingen**.

3   Can you show me **how to install this program**?
     Kannst du mir zeigen, **wie man dieses Programm installiert**?

     She asked me **where to put her dirty boots**.
     Sie fragte mich, **wo sie ihre schmutzigen Stiefel hinstellen sollte**.

LAS 4.1

1 a) (1) Coach told me my times **were** really good.
   (2) He said I **was** too slow.
   (3) Dad said I **could** use it while he **was** gone.

  c)

present	▶ **past**	"You are"	▶	… said I **was**
can	▶ *could*	"You can"	▶	… said I **could**
past	▶ **past perfect**	"You went"	▶	… said I **had gone**
present perfect	▶ **past perfect**	"You've done"	▶	… said I **had done**
will-**future**	▶ *would* + **infinitive**	"You'll see"	▶	… said I **would see**

3   (1) Drew said that **it was his dad's truck / his father's truck**.
     (2) Drew told Kaya that he **had watched her during practice**.
     (3) Kaya told Drew that **she didn't have a car**.
     (4) Drew answered that **he could drive her**.

LAS 4.2

1 a) (1) I asked him **whether** I **would make** the team.

(2) He asked **why** mom and I **lived** in Mobridge.

(3) He asked me **what** I **was doing** on the weekend.

(4) He asked **if** I **could go** to Mount Rushmore with him.

b) (1) Kaya: "**Will** I make the team?"

(2) Cody: "**Why do** you and your mom **live** in Mobridge?"

(3) Drew: "**What are** you **doing** on the weekend?"

(4) Drew: "**Can** you **come** with us?"

2

wh-questions	"Where's Kaya?"	►	He asked **where** Kaya was.
	"When do you usually have dinner?"	►	She asked **when** we usually had dinner.
Yes/No questions	"Are you OK?"	►	She wanted to know **if** (*or:* **whether**) I was OK.
	"Do you like cats?"	►	He wanted to know **if** (*or:* **whether**) I liked cats.

– When you report **wh-questions**, you keep the **question word** from the direct question.

– When you report **yes/no questions**, you need **if** or **whether**.

3 Jodi: "How long have you known him, Kaya?"

Jodi wanted to know **how long Kaya had known Drew**.

LAS 4.3

1 (1) Kaya: "My Aunt Jodi says Mount Rushmore is an insult to the Lakota people. She **told me not to go** there."

(2) Drew: "I **asked you to come** because I thought it would be fun."

– When you report **commands** (e.g. "Don't go there."), you use **tell sb. to do sth.**

– When you report **requests** (e.g. "Can you come with us?"), you use **ask sb. to do sth.**

2 Coach: "You should try to speed up a bit if you want to qualify, Kaya."

Coach **advised Kaya to speed up if she wanted to qualify.**

– When you report **advice**, you use **advise sb. to do sth.**

3 Bobby came up and **suggested going** for a pizza.

Bobby: "Hey Drew, **let's go** for a pizza."

When you want to report **suggestions**, you can use …

a **X suggested doing sth.**

b **X suggested that I/we do sth.**

d **X suggested I/we should do sth.**

LAS 4.4

1 b) – Nouns used in a **general sense** are used **without the definite article**.

– Nouns used in a **specific sense** are used **with the definite article**.

2 b) The nouns *church*, *hospital*, *prison*, *school*, *college*, *university* are used …

– **without the definite article** when we are talking about the **purpose** („Zweck") **of the building**.

– **with the definite article** when we are talking about the **building itself**.

LAS 5.1

1 b) You use   • **who** for people   • **which** for things   • **that** for people and things.

2   **"who"**-words: **guard, people, person, stranger, teenager, visitors**
     "which"-words: **banjo, city, magazine, national park, protests, whale**

3 a)   **correct:** sentences (1), (3), (4)   **wrong:** sentence (2)

   b) When the relative pronoun is the **object** of the relative clause as in sentence **3**, you can leave it out.
A relative clause without a relative pronoun is called "contact clause".
When the relative pronoun is the **subject** of the relative clause as in sentence **1**, you mustn't leave it out.

LAS 5.2

1 a) When I rang the bell, a woman **wearing high heels** answered the door.
Two teenagers **carrying big suitcases** walked up behind them.

   b) When I rang the bell, a woman **who was wearing high heels** answered the door.
Two teenagers **who were carrying big suitcases** walked up behind them.

2   **Participle clauses** (e.g. *a woman <u>wearing high heels</u>*) …   **a come directly after a noun.**
                                                          c can tell us what is or was happening.
                                                           d can be used instead of a relative clause.

3   Do you know the boy **playing the guitar**?
The dogs **fighting over the ball** are really cute.
Whose are all the shoes **lying around in the living room**?
The photo shows a woman **entering a bank**.
They picked up the rubbish **lying on the ground**.

LAS 5.3

1 a) We **watched a family of beavers swimming** in the river.
And Tyler **spotted a mule deer taking** a drink.
I **felt my grip tightening** on the paddle.
I **heard Dan calling** out our names.
Then I **saw** Julie **climbing** onto the overturned raft.

   b) If you want to say that you <u>feel, hear, notice, see, …</u> something that is (or was) going on,
you can use a **verb of perception + object + present participle**.

2   **Verbs of perception:** (to) **feel** • (to) **gaze** • (to) **hear** • (to) **listen to** • (to) **look at** • (to) **notice** • (to) **see** •
                                     (to) **smell** • (to) **spot** • (to) **watch**

3   There are a couple of dogs outside. I can **hear them barking**.
Can you **smell something burning**? Is there a fire?
Can you **hear** our neighbour's phone **ringing**? It makes me want to scream.
When we walked past the football pitch, we **noticed a man shouting** at some kids.

English G Access · Band 4
Vocabulary & Language Action Sheets

Kopiervorlagen mit Lösungen

Im Auftrag des Verlages herausgegeben von
Jörg Rademacher, Mannheim

Erarbeitet von
Dominik Eberhard, Bonn (Vocabulary Action Sheets)
Uwe Tröger, Hannover (Language Action Sheets)

Titelbild
Shutterstock, New York (Skyline): meunierd;
mauritius images, Mittenwald (Freiheitsstatue): imageBroker, Petra Wallner

Illustrationen
Vocabulary Action Sheets:
Roland Beier, Berlin
Language Action Sheets:
Tobias Dahmen, Utrecht/NL

Umschlaggestaltung
kleiner & bold, Berlin
hawemannundmosch, Berlin
klein & halm, Berlin

Layout und technische Umsetzung
zweiband.media, Berlin

www.cornelsen.de
www.englishg.de/access

1. Auflage, 1. Druck 2016

Alle Drucke dieser Auflage sind inhaltlich unverändert und
können im Unterricht nebeneinander verwendet werden.

© 2016 Cornelsen Verlag GmbH, Berlin

Druck: H. Heenemann, Berlin

ISBN 978-3-06-033496-4

PEFC zertifiziert
Dieses Produkt stammt aus nachhaltig
bewirtschafteten Wäldern und kontrollierten
Quellen.
www.pefc.de

PEFC/04-31-1156

Der clevere Assistent ...

Wortschatz wiederholen und festigen

Der *Wordmaster* ist ein vielfach bewährtes Arbeitsmittel, genau passend zum Schülerbuch: Er hilft dabei, sich neue Vokabeln nachhaltig einzuprägen, auch mit Rätseln oder Wortspielen.

Ein Lösungsheft liegt bei: So eignet sich das Heft sehr gut für die individuelle Arbeit zu Hause.

Ergo: Das ist doch bestimmt eine Empfehlung wert – an Ihre Achtklässler und deren Eltern ...

English G Access · Band 4
Wordmaster
Vokabelübungsheft mit Lösungen
56 Seiten, kartoniert
978-3-06-033083-6

... so smart!

Den aktuellen Preis und weitere Informationen finden Sie im Internet unter **www.englishg.de/access**

Cornelsen Verlag • 14328 Berlin

Willkommen in der Welt des Lernens